Puree for Baby

Puree for Baby

Jess Webster

Five Branch Publishing House
Atlanta, Georgia

Five Branch books can be ordered through booksellers.

ISBN: 978-0-615-35588-7 (sc)

Printed in the United States of America

Five Branch revision date 4/16/2010

For Holden and Honor Grace

Contents

Preface   xi

Introduction   xiii

   Benefits of Homemade Baby Food   xiii
   Preparation   xiv
      Steaming   xiv

      Pureeing   xv
   Freezing Guidelines   xv
   Reheating Guidelines   xvi
   Ingredient Notes   xvi

Fruits   1

   Apple Puree   3
   Apple and Rice Cereal   4
   Snow White's Apple   5
   Apple-Solutely-Berry Delicious   5
   Berry-Bana Apple   6
   Sweet Potatoed Apple   7
   Apple Chicken Bake   8
   Johnny Appleseed's Fixin's   9
   Squashed Apples   10
   Apple and Carrot   11
   Apple Noodle   12
   Apple and Apricot   13
   Avocado Puree   14
   Peach-cado   16
   Nana-cado   16
   Avocado and Pear   17
   Banana Puree   18
   Nana Grains   19
   Peary Banana   20

Banana and Peach   21
Sweetest Splendor   21
Banana, Peach, and Butternut Squash   22
'Nana Smoothie   22
Banana and Strawberry   23
Strawberry Banana Smoothie   23
Blueberry Puree   24
Breakfast Berries   25
Blueberry and Apple   26
Peary Berry   26
Bananaberry Smoothie   27
Blueberry Yogurt   27
Cantaloupe Puree   28
Morning Sunrise   29
Pearloupe   30
Good Morning Sunshine   31
Summer Surprise   32
Yum-Yum Smoothie   33
Peachy Apple   36
Peachy Pear   37
Peach Mango   38
Fruit Delight   39
Apple-Peach 'Nana   40
Peaches and Cream   41
Sweet Potatoes and Peaches   42
Squashed Peaches   43
Summer Supper   44
Peach and Apricot   45
Pear Puree   46
Pear and Rice Cereal   47
Mango-go Pears   48
Strawpeary   48
Pears, Strawberries and Apples, Oh My   49

Pear Dream   49
Butternut Pear   50
Plum Puree   50
Plummed Peach   51
Plum Berries   51
Plum Tucker   52
Plum Pudding   53
Prunes   54
Prunes and Pear   54
Prune 'Nana   55

Vegetables   57

Butternut Squash Puree   59
Bugs Bunny's Garden   60
Butternut Squash Chicken   61
Butternut Squash and Brown Rice   62
Butternut Squash Pasta   63
Pasta Supreme   64
Carrot Puree   65
Carrots and Corn   65
Peas and Carrots   66
Apricot Chicken   67
Carrot Chicken   68
Carrots with Brown Rice   68
Chicken and Veg   69
Carrots and Chicken with Brown Rice   70
Happy Harvest   71
Peter Pan's Garden   72
Sweet Potato Pea   73
Chicken Noodle   74
Sweet Potato Puree   74
Sweet 'Tato Squash   75
Sweet Potato and Apple with Peas   76

Sweet Potato Peaches   77
Pinocchio's Potatoes   78
Sweet Potato and Carrot   78
Sweet Potato and Peas   79
Sweet Greens   80
Sweet Potato Corn   81
Sweet Potato and Brown Rice   82
Sweet Savory Veggies   83
Sweet Potato Chicken   84
Sweet Apple Chicken   85
Mash Potatoes   86
Butternut Mashed Taters   86
Potato Corn Bake   87
White Potato with Peas   87
White Potato and Green Beans   88
Chicken and Taties   89
Tasty Taters   90
Summer Squash Puree   91
Summer Squash with Peas   91
Squish Squash Green Bean   92
Yummy Yellow Squash Chicken   93
Summer Squash and Brown Rice   94
Squashy Noodle   95

Preface

When I transitioned my son onto solid foods, I wanted to ensure a healthy and simple process. I researched commercial baby food and found that most of it was filled with preservatives and additives. I knew there had to be a healthier alternative for feeding my child. Luckily, I was in Australia at the time, where it is common to make homemade baby food. My mother-in-law introduced me to it, and I started creating my own food combinations. For easier preparation, my mother suggested freezing the food in batches. The simplicity of putting the purees in ice cube trays and freezing them for up to six weeks made my life easier and my son's healthier. As a mother I knew I was onto something amazing in being able to provide my child a homemade meal, as opposed to a packaged meal. When we traveled, I simply brought a few cubes in a microwave-safe dish and was able to feed my son anywhere. I found it rewarding to know exactly what was going into my child's food, and I liked that I could include a variety of foods.

I chose to steam my son's food to retain the most nutrients. The preparation was incredibly easy, and being able to freeze a majority of the recipes made the cooking even easier. The benefits of making my own baby food completely outweighed buying commercial. I couldn't understand why every parent wouldn't want to make their own baby food. Not only is making one's own baby food healthier, but it is less expensive. The benefits I have experienced through making homemade food for my baby I wanted to be able to share with parents and caregivers. I wanted to create a recipe book that used common fruits and vegetables like apples, bananas, sweet potatoes, and carrots—foods that can easily be used in cooking the rest of the family's meals. I wrote this group of recipes to share the process of making homemade baby food with others. I hope you find that it is rewarding, efficient, and inexpensive to feed your children fresh food made with love by their loved ones.

Introduction

Most babies are ready to start eating solid foods between the ages of four to six months, according to the American Academy of Pediatrics. At this age, a child's energy needs begin to increase, and solid food provides more calories as babies become more active. The AAP recommends giving a child one new food at a time and waiting two to three days before starting another in case of allergies. Many pediatricians recommend against giving young children fish or eggs because they believe allergic reactions are common. Although there is no evidence to support this recommendation, I have not included fish or eggs in any of the recipes. Most of the recipes in this book call for steaming; a method of cooking that allows food to retain the highest amount of nutrients. You may use boiling, baking, microwaving, or stewing instead when necessary. Each recipe specifies for what age child it is recommended, serving size, approximate preparation and cooking time, and whether or not it can be frozen.

Benefits of Homemade Baby Food

- Fresh, rich with nutrients and vitamins.

- Free of preservatives or additives.

- Quick and easy to prepare.

- Freezable, with storage time of up to 6 weeks.

- Homemade with love; parent/guardian knowledge of what ingredients go into child's food.

- Recipe combinations allow for using a variety of meals.

- Cost-effective to purchase fresh food and prepare one's self.

- Convenient for taking on the go and traveling.

- More suitable for cooking the same food for the entire family because the baby is introduced to a variety of foods.

- Tastes better! Canned and commercial baby foods lose nutrients as preservatives are added, which eliminates some of the flavor and leaves food bland and tasteless.

- Nutrient-rich, with breast milk, baby's regular milk, or supplement added to most of the purees.

Preparation

Steaming

Use the steam-cooking method when possible. It is the best cooking method for preserving nutrients and minerals.

Appliances used for steaming:

Food Steamer: Allows one to steam a variety of foods at once. A kitchen appliance used to prepare various foods in a sealed container that limits the escape of air and liquids at a preset pressure. A great tool for making batches.

Stainless steel expandable steamer: Affordable and easy to use in most cooking pans. Food is placed in center of the expandable steamer, in cooking pan, and placed over steam.

Double broiler: A double-decker cooking pan. The lower vessel holds the boiling water that provides steam. The upper vessel holds food to be steamed.

Rice steamer: Round steel ball with various small holes. This type of steamer is placed over steam from boiling water in a cooking pan. Electric rice steamers use a similar method for steaming and can be purchased as a unit.

Bamboo steamer: A stacked wok containing boiling water that provides steam for cooking.

Pureeing

- When choosing foods to puree, check the expiration date, when applicable, to ensure food is fresh. Inspect food to make sure it is not bruised. Wash thoroughly and remove debris.

- For babies who are just starting solids, purees should be very smooth in texture. As children get comfortable with texture, the purees can become thicker. Eventually a child will be able to eat food without pureeing.

- Use organic ingredients when possible.

Appliances used for pureeing:

Handheld mixer: An excellent tool for smaller servings; a handheld blender allows for quick and easy pureeing at various speeds.

Blender/Food Processor: Great for cooking in batches; an electric appliance that allows large amounts of food to be added and pureed at various levels of consistency.

Freezing Guidelines

- Food can be frozen in ice cube trays. Once it is frozen, pop the cubes out and store them in a freezer bag labeled with the contents and date the food was cooked.

- One cube from an ice cube container is approximately one ounce, or one serving.

- Freeze food once. Never re-freeze meals that have already been frozen. Only raw foods that have been cooked can be placed in the freezer. Large batches should be placed in the freezer as soon as food has cooled.

- Frozen baby purees will stay fresh for up to six weeks.

- Foods that have been cooked or frozen should only be placed in the refrigerator for up to 48 hours.

Reheating Guidelines

- When reheating purees, make sure that food is heated until thawed and hot; this will kill off any bacteria. Allow to cool before serving.

- Never reheat food more than once.

- Stir to eliminate hot spots and always check temperature before serving to make sure it is appropriate for your baby's mouth.

Ingredient Notes

- All of the recipes include a recommended cooking/preparation time and serving size. Due to variation of steamer/methods, food size, and storage, the cooking time and serving size may be different than suggested in the recipes.

- Peach/nectarine/plum preparation—to peel fruit: slit a small opening on base of fruit and place in boiling water for 45-60 seconds. Peel off flesh of fruit, discard, and use remainder of fruit for puree recipes.

- When choosing pasta: choose smaller size such as penne, fusilli, or macaroni. If you choose to use a larger pasta type, make sure to cook and puree thoroughly.

- Most of the purees call for 1-2 tablespoons of water to be used; however, you may substitute breast milk or baby's milk supplement for additional nutrients.

- Get creative! Try mixing and blending your child's favorite fruits and vegetables for their very own favorite puree!

Fruits

Apple Puree

1 medium-sized Braeburn, Gala, or Macintosh apple (peeled, cored, and chopped)

1 tablespoon water

1 tablespoon unsweetened apple juice for taste (optional)

Cook apple in steamer for 5-7 minutes, or until tender.

Blend apple and water until desired consistency is reached. Stir in apple juice, if using, and serve warm or cold.

*Appropriate age: 6 months

*Servings: 2-3

*Cooking time: 5-7 minutes

*Able to freeze

Apples contain a soluble fiber called pectin. This aids in regular movement of the digestive tract.

At 9-10 months, try adding toasted oats or plain Cheerios to the mixture and pureeing. This will give your baby additional vitamins and get them used to the texture of solid foods.

Apple and Rice Cereal

1 medium-sized apple (peeled, cored, and chopped)

¼ cup baby rice cereal

½ cup breast milk/baby's milk supplement

Cook apple in steamer for 5-7 minutes, or until tender.

Prepare rice cereal according to instructions on package.

Blend apple, rice cereal, and milk until a very smooth consistency is reached.

*Appropriate age: 6 months

*Servings: 5-7

*Cooking time: 5-7 minutes

*Able to freeze

At 7-9 months, substitute baby rice cereal for ¼ cup of rolled oats. Place oats and milk in cooking pan, and boil for 1 minute, let simmer for 4 minutes, blend with apple and puree.

For another breakfast treat, add raisins to the mixture by boiling ½ cup raisins in water for 5 minutes. Let soak and simmer for 30 minutes, drain water, add to the mixture, and puree.

Snow White's Apple

1 medium-sized apple (peeled, cored, and chopped)

1 banana (peeled)

1 tablespoon water

Cook apple in steamer for 5-7 minutes, or until tender.

Blend apple, banana, and water until desired consistency is reached.

*Appropriate age: 6 months

*Servings: 5-7

*Cooking time: 5-7 minutes

*Unable to freeze

Apple-Solutely-Berry Delicious

2 medium-sized apples (peeled, cored, and chopped)

¼ cup strawberries (stems removed), and quartered

1 tablespoon water

Cook apple in steamer for 5-7 minutes, or until tender.

Blend apples, strawberries, and water until desired consistency is achieved.

*Appropriate age: 11-12 months

*Servings: 8-10

*Cooking time: 5-7 minutes

*Able to freeze

Berry-Bana Apple

1 medium-sized apple (peeled, cored, and chopped)

¼ cup strawberries (stems removed), and quartered

1 banana (peeled)

1 tablespoon water

Cook apple in steamer for 5-7 minutes, or until tender.

Blend apple, strawberries, banana, and water until desired consistency is reached.

*Appropriate age: 11-12 months

*Servings: 10-12

*Cooking time: 5-7 minutes

*Unable to freeze

Sweet Potatoed Apple

1 medium-sized apple (peeled, cored, and chopped)

1 medium-sized sweet potato (peeled and chopped)

1 tablespoon water

1 pinch cinnamon (optional)

Cook apple in steamer for 5-7 minutes, or until tender.

Cook sweet potato in steamer for 16-18 minutes, or until tender.

Blend apple, sweet potato, and water until desired consistency is reached. At 8 months, stir in cinnamon for taste, and serve warm.

*Appropriate age: 6-8 months

*Servings: 6-8

*Cooking time: 16-18 minutes

*Able to freeze

Apple Chicken Bake

1 medium-sized apple (peeled, cored, and chopped)

1 chicken breast (boneless, skinless)

1 tablespoon water

2 tablespoons unsweetened apple juice for taste (optional)

Cook apple in steamer for 5-7 minutes, or until tender.

Place chicken in boiling water and boil for 12-14 minutes, or until cooked thoroughly.

Blend apple, chicken, and water until desired consistency is achieved. Stir in apple juice, if using.

*Appropriate age: 8-10 months

*Servings: 10-12

*Cooking time: 12-14 minutes

*Able to freeze

Johnny Appleseed's Fixin's

1 medium-sized apple (peeled, cored, and chopped)

2 medium-sized sweet potatoes (peeled and chopped)

1 chicken breast (boneless, skinless)

1 tablespoon water

Cook apple in steamer for 5-7 minutes, or until tender.

Cook sweet potatoes in steamer for 16-18 minutes, or until tender.

Place chicken in boiling water and boil for 12-14 minutes, or until cooked thoroughly.

Blend apple, sweet potatoes, chicken, and water until desired consistency is reached.

*Appropriate age: 8-10 months

*Servings: 10-12

*Cooking time: 16-18 minutes

*Able to freeze

Squashed Apples

3 medium-sized apples (peeled, cored, and chopped)

½ butternut squash (peeled, seeded, and cubed)

2 tablespoons water

Cook apple in steamer for 5-7 minutes, or until tender.

Cook butternut squash in steamer for 6-8 minutes, or until tender.

Blend apples, butternut squash, and water until a smooth consistency is reached.

*Appropriate age: 6-8 months

*Servings: 10-12

*Cooking time: 6-8 minutes

*Able to freeze

Apple and Carrot

1 medium-sized apple (peeled, cored, and chopped)

3 medium-sized carrots (peeled and sliced)

1 tablespoon water

1 tablespoon unsweetened apple juice for taste (optional)

Cook apple in steamer for 5-7 minutes, or until tender.

Cook carrots in steamer for 10-12 minutes, or until tender.

Blend apple, carrots, and water until desired consistency is reached. Stir in apple juice, if using.

*Appropriate age: 6-8 months

*Servings: 6-8

*Cooking time: 10-12 minutes

*Able to freeze

Apple Noodle

2 medium-sized apples (peeled, cored, and chopped)

½ cup dry pasta (of choice)

Cook apples in steamer for 5-7 minutes, or until tender.

Boil pasta in water for 8-10 minutes, or until pasta is tender. Drain excess water.

Blend apple, pasta, and water until desired consistency is achieved.

*Appropriate age: 7-9 months

*Servings: 6-8

*Cooking time: 8-10 minutes

*Able to freeze

Apple and Apricot

3 medium-sized Braeburn, Gala, or Macintosh apples (peeled, cored, and chopped)

4-6 dried apricots (chopped)

1 tablespoon water

Cook apricots in boiling water for 5 minutes, and let simmer for 10 minutes or until softened. Drain water.

Cook apple in steamer for 5-7 minutes, or until tender.

Blend apples, apricots and water until desired consistency is reached.

*Appropriate age: 9-12 months

*Servings: 10-12

*Cooking time: 15-17 minutes

*Able to freeze

Avocado Puree

1 avocado (cut lengthwise, with pit removed)

1 tablespoon water

Scoop avocado out of shell.

Mash avocado and water until a smooth consistency is achieved.

*Appropriate age: 6 months

*Servings: 1

*Cooking time: none

*Unable to freeze

At 9-10 months try adding toasted oats or plain Cheerios to the mixture, and puree. This will give your baby additional vitamins and get them used to the texture of solids.

Avocado and Rice Cereal

1 avocado (cut lengthwise, with pit removed)

½ cup baby rice cereal

¼ cup breast milk/baby's milk supplement

Prepare rice cereal according to instructions on package.

Scoop avocado out of peel.

Blend avocado, rice cereal and milk until smooth consistency is achieved.

*Appropriate age: 6-8 months

*Servings: 4-6

*Cooking time: 2-3 minutes

*Unable to freeze

Peach-cado

1 avocado (cut lengthwise, with pit removed)

1 peach (peeled, pitted, and sliced)

2 tablespoons water

Scoop avocado out of peel.

Cook peach in steamer for 6-8 minutes, or until tender.

Blend avocado, peach, and water until desired consistency is achieved.

*Appropriate age: 6-8 months

*Servings: 4-6

*Cooking time: 6-8 minutes

*Unable to freeze

Nana-cado

1 avocado (cut lengthwise, with pit removed)

1 banana (peeled)

1 tablespoon water

Scoop avocado out of peel.

Mash avocado, banana, and water until a smooth consistency achieved.

*Appropriate age: 6 months

*Servings: 4-6

*Cooking time: none

*Unable to freeze

Avocado and Pear

1 avocado (cut lengthwise, with pit removed)

1 pear (peeled, cored, and chopped)

1 tablespoon water

Cook pear in steamer for 4-6 minutes, or until tender.

Scoop avocado out of shell.

Blend avocado, pear, and water until desired consistency is achieved.

*Appropriate age: 6 months

*Servings: 4-6

*Cooking time: 4-6 minutes

*Unable to freeze

Banana Puree

1 banana (peeled)

¼ cup breast milk or baby's milk supplement (optional)

Blend banana until desired consistency is achieved.

*Appropriate age: 6 months

*Servings: 2-3

*Cooking time: none

*Unable to freeze

B is for banana—and vitamin B. Bananas are also high in potassium and fiber.

At 9-10 months, try adding toasted oats or plain Cheerios to the mixture, and puree. This will give your baby additional vitamins and get them used to the texture of solids.

Nana Grains

1 banana (peeled)

¼ cup baby rice cereal

½ cup breast milk/baby's milk supplement

Prepare rice cereal according to instructions on package.

Blend banana, rice cereal, milk until desired consistency is achieved.

*Appropriate age: 6 months

*Servings: 3-4

*Cooking time: 2-4 minutes

*Unable to freeze

At 7-9 months, substitute baby rice cereal for ¼ cup of rolled oats. Place oats and milk in cooking pan, and boil for 1 minute, let simmer for 4 minutes, blend with banana and puree.

Butternut Banana

2 bananas (peeled)

½ butternut squash (peeled, seeded, and cubed)

2 tablespoons water

Cook butternut squash in steamer for 6-8 minutes, or until tender.

Blend bananas, butternut squash, and water until desired consistency is achieved.

*Appropriate age: 6-8 months

*Servings: 10-12

*Cooking time: 6-8 minutes

*Unable to freeze

Peary Banana

1 banana (peeled)

1 pear (peeled, cored, and chopped)

Cook pear in steamer for 4-6 minutes, or until tender.

Blend banana and pear until desired consistency is reached.

*Appropriate age: 6 months

*Servings: 6-8

*Cooking time: 4-6 minutes

*Unable to freeze

Banana and Peach

1 banana (peeled)

1 peach (peeled, pitted, and sliced)

1 tablespoon water

 Cook peach in steamer for 6-8 minutes, or until tender.

 Blend banana, peach, and water until desired consistency is achieved.

*Appropriate age: 6-8 months

*Servings: 5-7

*Cooking time: 6-8 minutes

*Unable to freeze

Sweetest Splendor

1 banana (peeled)

1 peach (peeled, pitted, and sliced)

1 pear (peeled, cored, and chopped)

1 tablespoon water

Cook pear in steamer for 4-6 minutes, or until tender.

Cook peach in steamer for 6-8 minutes, or until tender.

Blend banana, pear, peach, and water until desired consistency is achieved.

*Appropriate age: 6-8 months

*Servings: 10-12

*Cooking time: 6-8 minutes

*Unable to freeze

Banana, Peach, and Butternut Squash

1 banana (peeled)

1 peach (peeled, pitted, and sliced)

½ butternut squash (peeled, seeded, and cubed)

1 tablespoon water

Steam peach and butternut squash for 6-8 minutes, or until tender.

Blend banana, peach, squash, and water until desired consistency is achieved.

*Appropriate age: 6-8 months

*Servings: 10-12

*Cooking time: 6-8 minutes

*Unable to freeze

'Nana Smoothie

1 banana (peeled)

3 tablespoons mild, whole milk, plain yogurt

Mash banana and mix with yogurt until desired consistency is reached.

*Appropriate age: 9-12 months

*Servings: 4-6

*Cooking time: none

*Unable to freeze

At 8-10 months, substitute the yogurt for silken tofu. Tofu is made from soybean-curd and is an excellent source of protein.

Banana and Strawberry

1 banana (peeled)

½ cup strawberries (stems removed), quartered

1 tablespoon water

Blend banana, strawberries, and water until desired consistency is achieved.

*Appropriate age: 11-12 months

*Servings: 5-7

*Cooking time: none

*Unable to freeze

Strawberry Banana Smoothie

1 banana (peeled)

½ cup strawberries (stems removed), quartered

3 tablespoons mild, whole milk, plain yogurt

Blend banana, strawberries, and yogurt until desired consistency is achieved.

*Appropriate age: 11-12 months

*Servings: 6-8

*Cooking time: none

*Unable to freeze

At 8-10 months, substitute the yogurt for silken tofu. Tofu is made from soybean-curd and is an excellent source of protein.

This is my son's favorite puree, and when I added tofu for additional nutrients, he wasn't able to tell much of a difference in taste!

Blueberry Puree

½ cup blueberries

3 tablespoons breast milk/baby's milk supplement

Gently steam blueberries for 3-5 minutes, or until tender.

Blend blueberries and milk until smooth consistency is reached.

*Appropriate age: 8-10 months

*Servings: 3-4

*Cooking time: 3-5 minutes

*Able to freeze

Blueberries are an excellent source of vitamin C, K, and manganese.

Breakfast Berries

½ cup blueberries

¼ cup baby rice cereal

½ cup breast milk/baby's milk supplement.

Gently steam blueberries for 3-5 minutes, or until tender.

Prepare rice cereal according to instructions on package.

Blend blueberries, rice cereal, and breast milk/baby's milk supplement until desired consistency is achieved.

*Appropriate age: 8-10 months

*Servings: 4-6

*Cooking time: 3-5 minutes

*Able to freeze

At 7-9 months, substitute baby rice cereal for ¼ cup of rolled oats. Place oats and milk in cooking pan, and boil for 1 minute, let simmer for 4 minutes, blend with blueberries and puree.

Blueberry and Apple

½ cup blueberries

1 medium-sized apple (peeled, cored, and chopped)

1 tablespoon water

Gently steam blueberries for 3-5 minutes, or until tender.

Cook apple in steam for 5-7 minutes, or until tender.

Blend blueberries, apple, and water until desired consistency is achieved.

*Appropriate age: 9-12 months

*Servings: 6-8

*Cooking time: 5-7 minutes

*Able to freeze

Peary Berry

½ cup blueberries

1 pear (peeled, cored, and chopped)

Gently steam blueberries for 3-5 minutes, or until tender.

Cook pears in steamer for 4-6 minutes, or until tender. Blend blueberries and pear until desired level of consistency is achieved.

*Appropriate age: 9-12 months

*Servings: 4-6

*Cooking time: 4-6 minutes

*Able to freeze

Optional: Add apple puree to the mixture for an even sweeter taste and an additional 2 servings.

Bananaberry Smoothie

½ cup blueberries

1 banana (peeled)

3 tablespoons mild, whole milk, plain yogurt

Gently steam blueberries for 3-5 minutes, or until tender.

Blend blueberries, banana, and yogurt until desired consistency is achieved.

*Appropriate age: 9-12 months

*Servings: 6-8

*Cooking time: 3-5 minutes

*Unable to freeze

At 8-10 months, substitute the yogurt for silken tofu. Tofu is made from soybean-curd and is an excellent source of protein.

Blueberry Yogurt

½ cup blueberries

3 tablespoons mild, whole milk plain yogurt

Gently steam blueberries for 3-5 minutes, or until tender.

Blend blueberries and yogurt until desired consistency is achieved.

*Appropriate age: 9-12 months

*Servings: 3-4

*Cooking time: 3-5 minutes

*Able to freeze

Before freezing, place a baby-safe plastic spoon in the center. These frozen yogurt cubes can become yummy handheld popsicles at 11-12 months.

Cantaloupe Puree

½ cantaloupe (seeded)

1 tablespoon water

Scoop cantaloupe from shell.

Blend cantaloupe and water until smooth consistency is reached.

*Appropriate age: 8-10 months

*Servings: 4-6

*Cooking time: none

*Unable to freeze

Puree can be stored in refrigerator for up to 48 hours.

Honeydew melon may be used as a substitute for cantaloupe.

Cantaloupe is a good source of dietary fiber, niacin, folate, potassium, and vitamins A, B, and C.

Morning Sunrise

½ cantaloupe (seeded)

¼ cup baby rice cereal

½ cup breast milk/baby's milk supplement

Scoop cantaloupe from shell.

Prepare rice cereal according to instructions on package.

Blend cantaloupe, rice cereal, and milk until desired level of consistency is achieved.

*Appropriate age: 8-10 months

*Servings: 7-9

*Cooking time: 4-6 minutes

*Unable to freeze

At 7-9 months, substitute baby rice cereal for ¼ cup of rolled oats. Place oats and milk in cooking pan, and boil for 1 minute, let simmer for 4 minutes, blend with cantaloupe and puree.

Pearloupe

½ cantaloupe (seeded)

2 pears (peeled, cored, and chopped)

1 tablespoon water

Cook pears in steamer for 4-6 minutes, or until tender.

Scoop cantaloupe from shell.

Blend cantaloupe, pears, and water until desired consistency is achieved.

*Appropriate age: 8-10 months

*Servings: 10-12

*Cooking time: 4-6 minutes

*Unable to freeze

Puree can be stored in refrigerator for up to 48 hours.

Good Morning Sunshine

½ cantaloupe (seeded)

2 peaches (peeled, pitted, and chopped)

1 tablespoon water

Cook peaches in steamer for 6-8 minutes, or until tender.

Scoop cantaloupe from shell.

Blend cantaloupe, peaches, and water until desired consistency is achieved.

*Appropriate age: 8-10 months

*Servings: 10-12

*Cooking time: 6-8 minutes

*Unable to freeze

Puree can be stored in refrigerator for up to 48 hours.

Summer Surprise

½ cantaloupe (seeded)

1 banana (peeled)

1 pear (peeled, cored, and chopped)

1 tablespoon water

Cook pear in steamer for 4-6 minutes, or until tender.

Scoop cantaloupe from shell.

Blend cantaloupe, banana, pear, and water until desired consistency is achieved.

*Appropriate age: 8-10 months

*Servings: 10-12

*Cooking time: 4-6 minutes

*Unable to freeze

Yum-Yum Smoothie

½ cantaloupe (seeded)

½ cup mild, whole milk plain yogurt

Scoop cantaloupe from shell.

Blend cantaloupe and yogurt until desired consistency is achieved.

*Appropriate age: 9-12 months

*Servings: 4-6

*Cooking time: none

*Unable to freeze

Puree can be stored in refrigerator for up to 48 hours.

At 8-10 months, substitute the yogurt for silken tofu. Tofu is made from soybean-curd and is an excellent source of protein.

Peach Puree

1 peach (peeled, pitted and sliced)

1 tablespoon water

Cook peach in steamer for 6-8 minutes, or until tender.

Blend peach and water until desired consistency is achieved.

*Appropriate age: 6 months

*Servings: 2-3

*Cooking time: 6-8 minutes

*Able to freeze

Peaches are an excellent source of vitamins A, C, E, K, and niacin.

Nectarines may be used as a substitute for peaches.

Peach and Rice Cereal

1 peach (peeled, pitted, and sliced)

¼ cup baby rice cereal

½ cup breast milk/baby's milk supplement

Cook peach in steamer for 6-8 minutes, or until tender.

Prepare rice cereal according to instructions on package.

Blend peach, rice cereal and milk until desired level of consistency is achieved.

*Appropriate age: 6-8 months

*Servings: 3-4

*Cooking time: 4-6 minutes

*Able to freeze

At 7-9 months, substitute baby rice cereal for ¼ cup of rolled oats. Place oats and milk in cooking pan, and boil for 1 minute, let simmer for 4 minutes, blend with peach and puree.

Peachy Apple

1 peach (peeled, pitted, and sliced)

1 medium-sized apple (peeled, cored, and chopped)

1 tablespoon water

1 pinch of cinnamon (optional)

Cook peach in steamer for 6-8 minutes, or until tender.

Cook apple in steamer for 5-7 minutes, or until tender.

Blend peach, apple, and water until desired consistency is achieved. Stir in cinnamon, if using, and serve warm or cold.

*Appropriate age: 6-8 months

*Servings: 4-6

*Cooking time: 6-8 minutes

*Able to freeze

Peachy Pear

2 peaches (peeled, pitted, and sliced)

2 pears (peeled, cored, and chopped)

1 tablespoon water

Cook peaches in steamer for 6-8 minutes, or until tender.

Cook pears in steamer for 5-7 minutes, or until tender.

Blend peaches, pears, and water until desired consistency is achieved.

*Appropriate age: 6 months

*Servings: 6-8

*Cooking time: 6-8 minutes

*Able to freeze

Peach Mango

1 peach (peeled, pitted, and sliced)

1 mango (peeled, pit removed, and chopped)

1 tablespoon water

Steam peach and mango for 6-8 minutes, or until tender.

Blend peach, mango, and water until desired consistency is achieved.

*Appropriate age: 8-10 months

*Servings: 4-6

*Cooking time: 6-8 minutes

*Able to freeze

You may substitute the mango for dried mango. Place ½ cup of dried mango in boiling water for 5 minutes, and let simmer for 15 minutes. Drain water, add to mixture and puree.

Fruit Delight

1 peach (peeled, pitted, and sliced)

1 medium-sized apple (peeled, cored, and chopped)

¼ cup strawberries (stems removed), and quartered

1 tablespoon water

Cook peach in steamer for 6-8 minutes, or until tender.

Cook apple in steamer for 5-7 minutes, or until tender.

Blend peach, apple, strawberries, and water until desired consistency is achieved.

*Appropriate age: 11-12 months

*Servings: 6-8

*Cooking time: 6-8 minutes

*Able to freeze

This is a great puree to introduce a variety of fruits that offer a range of nutrients and minerals.

Apple-Peach 'Nana

1 peach (peeled, pitted, and sliced)

1 medium-sized apple (peeled, cored, and chopped)

1 banana (peeled)

1 tablespoon water

Cook peach in steamer for 6-8 minutes, or until tender.

Cook apple in steamer for 5-7 minutes, or until tender.

Blend peach, apple, banana, and water until desired consistency is achieved.

*Appropriate age: 6-8 months

*Servings: 6-8

*Cooking time: 6-8 minutes

*Unable to freeze

Peaches and Cream

1 peach (peeled, pitted, and sliced)

3 tablespoons mild, whole milk plain yogurt

Cook peach in steamer for 6-8 minutes, or until tender.

Blend peach and yogurt until desired consistency is achieved.

*Appropriate age: 9-12 months

*Servings: 4-6

*Cooking time: 6-8 minutes

*Able to freeze

Before freezing, place a baby-safe plastic spoon in the center of each cube. These frozen yogurt cubes can become yummy popsicles at 11-12 months.

At 8-10 months, substitute the yogurt for silken tofu. Tofu is made from soybean-curd and is an excellent source of protein.

Sweet Potatoes and Peaches

2 peaches (peeled, pitted, and sliced)

2 sweet potatoes (peeled and chopped)

Cook peaches in steamer for 6-8 minutes, or until tender.

Steam sweet potatoes for 16-18 minutes or until tender.

Blend peaches, sweet potatoes, and water until desired consistency is achieved.

*Appropriate age: 6-8 months

*Servings: 6-8

*Cooking time: 16-18 minutes

*Able to freeze

Squashed Peaches

3 peaches (peeled, pitted, and sliced)

½ butternut squash (peeled, seeded, cubed)

1 tablespoon water

Cook peaches and squash in steamer for 6-8 minutes, or until tender.

Blend peaches, squash, and water until desired consistency is achieved.

*Appropriate age: 6-8 months

*Servings: 10-12

*Cooking time: 6-8 minutes

*Able to freeze

Summer Supper

2 peaches (peeled, pitted, and sliced)

1 chicken breast (boneless, skinless)

1 tablespoon water

Cook peaches in steamer for 6-8 minutes, or until tender.

Cook chicken in boiling water for 12-14 minutes, or until cooked thoroughly.

Blend peaches, chicken, and water until desired consistency is achieved.

*Appropriate age: 8-10 months

*Servings: 10-12

*Cooking time: 12-14 minutes

*Able to freeze

Adding sweet fruit, such as peaches, to chicken makes the protein tastier for your baby and eases the transition!

Peach and Apricot

1 peach (peeled, pitted and sliced)

4-6 dried apricots (chopped)

1 tablespoon water

Cook apricots in boiling water for 5 minutes, and let simmer for 10 minutes or until softened. Drain water.

Cook peach in steamer for 6-8 minutes, or until tender.

Blend peach, apricots, and water until desired consistency is achieved.

*Appropriate age: 6 months

*Servings: 4-6

*Cooking time: 15-17 minutes

*Able to freeze

Peaches are an excellent source of vitamins A, C, E, K, and niacin.

Nectarines may be used as a substitute for peaches.

Pear Puree

1 pear (peeled, cored, and chopped)

Cook pear in steamer for 4-6 minutes, or until tender.

Blend pear until desired level of consistency is achieved.

*Appropriate age: 6 months

*Servings: 2-3

*Cooking time: 4-6 minutes

*Able to freeze

Pears are a great source of vitamin C.

Pear and Rice Cereal

1 pear (peeled, cored, and chopped)

¼ cup baby rice cereal

½ cup breast milk/baby's milk supplement

Cook pear in steamer for 4-6 minutes, or until tender.

Prepare rice cereal according to instructions on package.

Blend pear, rice cereal, and milk until desired level of consistency is achieved.

*Appropriate age: 6 months

*Servings: 4-6

*Cooking time: 4-6 minutes

*Able to freeze

At 7-9 months, substitute baby rice cereal for ¼ cup of rolled oats. Place oats and milk in cooking pan, and boil for 1 minute, let simmer for 4 minutes, blend with pear and puree.

For another breakfast treat, add raisins in water to the mixture by boiling ½ cup raisins to boiling water for 5 minutes. Let soak and simmer for 5 minutes, drain water, add to the mixture, and puree.

Mango-go Pears

2 pears (peeled, cored, and chopped)

1 mango (peeled, pit removed, and chopped)

1 tablespoon water

Cook pears and mango in steamer for 4-6 minutes, or until tender.

Blend pears, mango, and water until desired consistency is achieved.

*Appropriate age: 8-10 months

*Servings: 7-9

*Cooking time: 4-6 minutes

*Able to freeze

Strawpeary

1 pear (peeled, cored, and chopped)

¼ cup strawberries (stems removed), and quartered

Cook pear in steamer for 4-6 minutes or until tender.

Blend pear and strawberries until desired consistency is achieved.

*Appropriate age: 11-12 months

*Servings: 4-6

*Cooking time: 4-6 minutes

*Able to freeze

Pears, Strawberries and Apples, Oh My

1 pear (peeled, cored, and chopped)

¼ cup strawberries (stems removed), and quartered

1 apple (peeled, cored, and chopped)

1 tablespoon water

Place pear and apple in steamer, and steam for 5-7 minutes or until tender.

Blend pear, strawberries, apple, and water until desired consistency is achieved.

*Appropriate age: 11-12 months

*Servings: 6-8

*Cooking time: 5-7 minutes

*Able to freeze

Pear Dream

1 pear (peeled, cored, and chopped)

3 tablespoons of mild, whole milk plain yogurt

Cook pear in steamer for 5-7 minutes or until tender.

Blend pear and yogurt until desired consistency is achieved.

*Appropriate age: 10-12 months

*Servings: 3-5

*Cooking time: 5-7 minutes

*Able to freeze

Before freezing, place a baby-safe, plastic spoon in the center of each cube. These frozen yogurt cubes can become yummy popsicles at 11-12 months.

Butternut Pear

3 pears (peeled, cored, and chopped)

½ butternut squash (peeled, seeded, and cubed)

Cook pears in steamer for 5-7 minutes, or until tender.

Cook squash in steamer for 6-8 minutes, or until tender.

Blend pears and squash until desired consistency is achieved.

*Appropriate age: 6-8 months

*Servings: 10-12

*Cooking time: 6-8 minutes

*Able to freeze

Plum Puree

2 plums (peeled, pitted, and cubed)

2 tablespoons water

Gently steam plums in steamer for 3-5 minutes, or until tender.

Blend plums and water until desired consistency is achieved.

*Appropriate age: 6-8 months

*Servings: 2-3

*Cooking time: 3-5 minutes

*Able to freeze

Plums are a good source of vitamin K, and dietary fiber. Prunes and Plums aid in digestion.

Plummed Peach

1 plum (peeled, pitted, and cubed)

1 peach (peeled, pitted, and sliced)

1 tablespoon water

Gently steam plum in steamer for 3-5 minutes, or until tender.

Steam peach for 6-8 minutes, or until tender.

Blend plum, peach, and water until desired consistency is achieved.

*Appropriate age: 6-8 months

*Servings: 5-7

*Cooking time: 6-8 minutes

*Able to freeze

Plum Berries

1 plum (peeled, pitted, and cubed)

½ cup blueberries

1 tablespoon water

Place plum and blueberries in steamer, and steam for 3-5 minutes, or until tender.

Blend plum, blueberries, and water until desired consistency is achieved.

*Appropriate age: 9-11 months

*Servings: 4-6

*Cooking time: 3-5 minutes

*Able to freeze

Plum Tucker

3 plums (peeled, pitted, and cubed)

1 chicken breast (boneless, skinless)

2 tablespoons water

Gently steam plums for 3-5 minutes, or until tender.

Cook chicken in boiling water for 12-14 minutes, or until cooked thoroughly.

Blend plums, chicken, and water until desired consistency is achieved.

*Appropriate age: 8-10 months

*Servings: 8-10

*Cooking time: 12-14 minutes

*Able to freeze

Plum Pudding

1 plum (peeled, pitted, and cubed)

1 peach (peeled, pitted, and sliced)

3 tablespoons mild, whole milk plain yogurt

1 tablespoon water

Gently steam plums for 3-5 minutes, or until tender.

Cook peach in steamer for 6-8 minutes, or until tender.

Blend plum, peach, yogurt, and water until desired consistency is achieved.

*Appropriate age: 8-10 months

*Servings: 6-8

*Cooking time: 6-8 minutes

*Able to freeze

Before freezing, place a baby-safe, plastic spoon in the center of each cube. These frozen yogurt cubes can become yummy popsicles at 11-12 months.

Prunes

½ cup dried prunes

3 tablespoons water

Steam prunes for 4-6 minutes, or until tender.

Blend prunes and water until desired consistency is achieved.

*Appropriate age: 6 months

*Servings: 2

*Cooking time: 4-6 minutes

*Unable to freeze

Prunes are an excellent source of dietary fiber.

Prunes and Pear

½ cup dried prunes

1 pear (peeled, cored, and chopped)

3 tablespoons water

Steam prunes for 4-6 minutes, or until tender.

Steam pear for 5-7 minutes, or until tender.

Blend prunes, pear, and water until desired consistency is achieved.

*Appropriate age: 6 months

*Servings: 5-7

*Cooking time: 5-7 minutes

*Unable to freeze

Prune 'Nana

½ cup dried prunes

1 banana (peeled)

2 tablespoons water

Steam prunes for 4-6 minutes, or until tender.

Mash prunes, banana, and water until smooth consistency is achieved.

*Appropriate age: 6 months

*Servings: 6-8

*Cooking time: 4-6 minutes

*Unable to freeze

Vegetables

Butternut Squash Puree

½ butternut squash (peeled, seeded, and cubed)

2 tablespoons water

1 pinch of cinnamon to taste (optional)

Cook butternut squash in steamer for 6-8 minutes, or until tender.

Blend squash and water until desired consistency is achieved. Stir in cinnamon, if using, and serve warm.

*Appropriate age: 6-8 months

*Servings: 6-8

*Cooking time: 6-8 minutes

*Able to freeze

Butternut squash is a good source of vitamins A, C, E, thiamin, niacin, folate, calcium, magnesium, potassium, and manganese.

Acorn squash may be substituted for butternut squash.

Try planting your own vegetable garden for fresh vegetables!

Bugs Bunny's Garden

½ butternut squash (peeled, seeded, and cubed)

6 medium-sized carrots (peeled and diced)

2 tablespoons water

Cook squash in steamer for 6-8 minutes, or until tender.

Steam carrots for 10-12 minutes, or until tender.

Blend butternut squash, carrots, and water until desired consistency is achieved.

*Appropriate age: 6-8 months

*Servings: 10-12

*Cooking time: 10-12 minutes

*Able to freeze

Butternut Squash Chicken

½ butternut squash (peeled, seeded, and cubed)

1 chicken breast (boneless, skinless)

2 tablespoons water

Cook squash in steamer for 6-8 minutes, or until tender.

Cook chicken in boiling water for 12-14 minutes, or until cooked thoroughly.

Blend butternut squash, chicken, and water until desired consistency is achieved.

*Appropriate age: 10-12 months

*Servings: 10-12

*Cooking time: 12-14 minutes

*Able to freeze

Butternut Squash and Brown Rice

½ butternut squash (peeled, seeded, and cubed)

¼ cup brown rice

1 tablespoon water

Cook squash in steamer for 6-8 minutes, or until tender.

Cook rice in boiling water for 5 minutes. Reduce heat and simmer for 15 minutes, or until rice is tender.

Blend butternut squash, brown rice, and water until desired consistency is achieved.

*Appropriate age: 10-12 months

*Servings: 8-10

*Cooking time: 20 minutes

*Unable to freeze

Butternut Squash Pasta

½ butternut squash (peeled, seeded, and cubed)

½ cup dry pasta (of choice)

Cook squash in steamer for 6-8 minutes, or until tender.

Cook pasta in boiling water for 8-10 minutes, or until pasta is tender. Drain excess water.

Blend butternut squash and pasta until desired consistency is achieved.

*Appropriate age: 10-12 months

*Servings: 10-12

*Cooking time: 8-10 minutes

*Able to freeze

Pasta Supreme

½ butternut squash (peeled, seeded, and cubed)

½ cup dry pasta (of choice)

1 chicken breast (boneless, skinless)

2 tablespoons water

Cook squash in steamer for 6-8 minutes, or until tender.

Cook pasta in boiling water for 8-10 minutes, or until pasta is tender. Drain excess water.

Cook chicken in boiling water for 12-14 minutes, or until cooked thoroughly.

Blend squash, chicken, pasta, and water until desired consistency is achieved.

*Appropriate age: 10-12 months

*Servings: 10-12

*Cooking time: 12-14 minutes

*Able to freeze

Carrot Puree

6 medium-sized carrots (peeled and diced)

1 tablespoon water

Cook carrots in steamer for 10-12 minutes, or until tender.

Blend carrots and water until desired consistency is achieved.

*Appropriate age: 6 months

*Servings: 4-6

*Cooking time: 10-12 minutes

*Able to freeze

Carrots are a good source of vitamin A, E, K, dietary fiber, and potassium.

Carrots and Corn

6 medium-sized carrots (peeled and diced)

3 ears of corn (cut corn from cob) or ½ cup of frozen corn kernels

1 tablespoon water

Steam carrots for 10-12 minutes, or until tender.

Cook corn in steamer for 8-10 minutes, or until tender.

Blend carrots, corn, and water until desired consistency is achieved.

*Appropriate age: 10-12 months

*Servings: 10-12

*Cooking time: 10-12 minutes

*Able to freeze

Peas and Carrots

6 medium-sized carrots (peeled and diced)

1 cup frozen peas or 1 cup fresh peas (pulled from pod)

1 tablespoon water

Steam carrots for 10-12 minutes, or until tender.

Cook peas in steamer for 4-6 minutes, or until tender.

Blend carrots, peas, and water until desired consistency is achieved.

*Appropriate age: 7-9 months

*Servings: 10-12

*Cooking time: 10-12 minutes

*Able to freeze

Apricot Chicken

6 medium-sized carrots (peeled and diced)

1 chicken breast (boneless, skinless)

½ cup dried apricots (chopped)

1 tablespoon water

Cook apricots in boiling water for 5 minutes, and let simmer for 15 minutes or until softened. Drain water.

Steam carrots for 10-12 minutes, or until tender.

Cook chicken in boiling water for 12-14 minutes, or until cooked thoroughly.

Blend carrots, chicken, apricots, and water until desired consistency is achieved.

*Appropriate age: 8-10 months

*Servings: 10-12

*Cooking time: 20-22 minutes

*Able to freeze

You may use fresh apricots in this recipe. Using 2 apricots, remove peel, core and chop. Steam for 5-7 minutes, add to mixture and puree.

My husband gave me the idea for this recipe; one of his favorite meals is Apricot Chicken. I added carrot to create a full course meal in this puree.

Carrot Chicken

6 medium-sized carrots (peeled and diced)

1 chicken breast (boneless, skinless)

1 tablespoon water

Steam carrots for 10-12 minutes, or until tender.

Cook chicken in boiling water for 12-14 minutes, or until cooked thoroughly.

Blend carrots, chicken, and water until desired consistency is achieved.

*Appropriate age: 8-10 months

*Servings: 10-12

*Cooking time: 12-14 minutes

*Able to freeze

Carrots with Brown Rice

3 medium-sized carrots (peeled and diced)

¼ cup brown rice

2 tablespoons water

Steam carrots for 10-12 minutes, or until tender.

Cook rice in boiling water for 5 minutes. Simmer for 15 minutes, or until rice is tender.

Blend carrots, rice, and water until desired consistency is achieved.

*Appropriate age: 8-10 months

*Servings: 8-10

*Cooking time: 20 minutes

*Unable to freeze

Chicken and Veg

6 medium-sized carrots (peeled and diced)

1 chicken breast (boneless, skinless)

1 cup frozen peas or 1 cup fresh peas (removed from pod)

2 tablespoons water

1 clove garlic (crushed), optional

Steam carrots for 10-12 minutes, or until tender.

Cook chicken in boiling water for 12-14 minutes, or until cooked thoroughly.

Steam peas for 4-6 minutes, or until tender.

Blend carrots, chicken, peas, and water until desired consistency is achieved. Stir in garlic, if using, at 9 months for additional taste.

*Appropriate age: 8-10 months

*Servings: 12+

*Cooking time: 12-14 minutes

*Able to freeze

Carrots and Chicken with Brown Rice

6 medium-sized carrots (peeled and diced)

1 chicken breast (boneless, skinless)

¼ cup brown rice

2 tablespoons water

Steam carrots for 10-12 minutes, or until tender.

Cook chicken in boiling water for 12-14 minutes, or until cooked thoroughly.

Cook rice in boiling water for 5 minutes. Reduce heat and simmer for 15 minutes, or until rice is tender.

Blend carrots, chicken, brown rice, and water until desired consistency is achieved.

*Appropriate age: 8-10 months

*Servings: 10-12

*Cooking time: 20 minutes

*Unable to freeze

Happy Harvest

6 medium-sized carrots (peeled and diced)

1 chicken breast (boneless, skinless)

1 cup frozen green beans or 1 cup fresh green beans (topped, tailed, and chopped)

1 tablespoon water

Steam carrots for 10-12 minutes, or until tender.

Cook chicken in boiling water for 12-14 minutes, or until thoroughly cooked.

Steam green beans for 8-10 minutes, or until tender.

Blend carrots, chicken, green beans, and water until desired consistency is achieved.

*Appropriate age: 8-10 months

*Servings: 12+

*Cooking time: 12-14 minutes

*Able to freeze

For a tastier meal, add apricots! Cook ½ cup dried apricots in boiling water for 5 minutes, and let simmer for 15 minutes or until softened. Drain water. Add to mixture and puree.

Peter Pan's Garden

3 medium-sized carrots (peeled and diced)

1 white potato (peeled and chopped)

1 cup frozen peas or 1 cup fresh peas (removed from pod)

1 clove garlic (crushed), optional

2 tablespoons water

Steam carrots for 10-12 minutes, or until tender.

Steam white potato for 16-18 minutes, or until tender.

Steam peas for 4-6 minutes, or until tender.

Blend carrots, potatoes, peas, and water until desired consistency is achieved. Stir in garlic, if using, for additional taste.

*Appropriate age: 8-10 months

*Servings: 10-12

*Cooking time: 16-18 minutes

*Able to freeze

Sweet Potato Pea

3 medium-sized carrots (peeled and diced)

1 medium-sized sweet potato (peeled and chopped)

1 cup frozen peas or 1 cup fresh peas (removed from pod)

2 tablespoons water

1 clove garlic (crushed), optional

Steam carrots for 10-12 minutes, or until tender.

Steam sweet potatoes for 16-18 minutes, or until tender.

Steam peas for 4-6 minutes, or until tender.

Blend carrots, sweet potato, peas, and water until desired consistency is achieved. Stir in garlic, if using, for additional taste.

*Appropriate age: 8-10 months

*Servings: 10-12

*Cooking time: 16-18 minutes

*Able to freeze

Chicken Noodle

6 medium-sized carrots (peeled and diced)

1 chicken breast (boneless, skinless)

½ cup dry pasta (of choice)

Steam carrots for 10-12 minutes or until tender.

Cook chicken in boiling water for 12-14 minutes, or until thoroughly cooked.

Cook pasta in boiling water for 8-10 minutes, or until pasta is tender. Drain excess water.

Blend carrot, chicken, and pasta until desired consistency is achieved.

*Appropriate age: 8-10 months

*Servings: 12+

*Cooking time: 12-14 minutes

*Able to freeze

Sweet Potato Puree

1 medium-sized sweet potato (peeled and chopped)
1 tablespoon water
Steam sweet potato for 16-18 minutes or until tender.
Blend sweet potato and water until desired level of consistency is achieved.
*Appropriate age: 8-10 months

*Servings: 12+

*Cooking time: 12-14 minutes

*Able to freeze

At 9-10 months, try adding toasted oats or plain Cheerios to the mixture and pureeing.

Sweet 'Tato Squash

1 medium-sized sweet potato (peeled and chopped)

½ butternut squash (peeled, seeded, and cubed)

2 tablespoons water

Steam sweet potatoes for 16-18 minutes, or until tender.

Steam butternut squash for 6-8 minutes, or until tender.

Blend sweet potato, squash, and water until desired consistency is achieved.

*Appropriate age: 6-8 months

*Servings: 8-10

*Cooking time: 16-18 minutes

*Able to freeze

Sweet potatoes are a great source of dietary fiber, vitamin A, B, C, and manganese.

Sweet Potato and Apple with Peas

1 medium-sized sweet potato

1 apple (peeled, cored, and chopped)

1 cup frozen peas or 1 cup fresh peas (removed from pod)

1 tablespoon water

Steam sweet potato for 16-18 minutes, or until tender.

Steam apple for 5-7 minutes, or until tender.

Steam peas for 4-6 minutes, or until tender.

Blend sweet potato, apple, peas, and water until desired consistency is achieved.

*Appropriate age: 8-12 months

*Servings: 12+

*Cooking time: 16-18 minutes

*Able to freeze

Sweet Potato Peaches

1 medium-sized sweet potato (peeled and chopped)

1 peach (peeled, pitted, and sliced)

1 tablespoon of water

Steam sweet potatoes for 16-18 minutes, or until tender.

Steam peaches for 6-8 minutes, or until tender.

Blend sweet potato, peach, and water until desired consistency is achieved.

*Appropriate age: 6 months

*Servings: 6-8

*Cooking time: 16-18 minutes

*Able to freeze

Pinocchio's Potatoes

2 medium-sized sweet potatoes (peeled and chopped)

2 medium-sized white potatoes (peeled and chopped)

1 tablespoon of water

Steam sweet potatoes and white potatoes for 16-18 minutes, or until tender.

Blend sweet potatoes, white potatoes, and water until desired consistency is achieved.

*Appropriate age: 6 months

*Servings: 6-8

*Cooking time: 16-18 minutes

*Able to freeze

Sweet Potato and Carrot

1 medium-sized sweet potato (peeled and chopped)

3 medium-sized carrots (peeled and diced)

1 tablespoon water

Steam sweet potatoes for 16-18 minutes, or until tender.

Steam carrots for 10-12 minutes, or until tender.

Blend sweet potato, carrot, and water until desired consistency is achieved.

*Appropriate age: 6 months

*Servings: 8-12

*Cooking time: 16-18 minutes

*Able to freeze

Sweet Potato and Peas

2 medium-sized sweet potatoes (peeled and chopped)

1 cup frozen peas or 1 cup fresh peas (removed from pod)

1 tablespoon of water

Steam sweet potatoes for 16-18 minutes, or until tender.

Steam peas for 4-6 minutes, or until tender.

Blend sweet potatoes, peas, and water until desired consistency is achieved.

*Appropriate age: 8-10 months

*Servings-10-12

*Cooking time: 16-18 minutes

*Able to freeze

Sweet Greens

2 medium-sized sweet potatoes (peeled and chopped)

1 cup frozen green beans or 1 cup fresh (topped, tailed, and chopped)

1 tablespoon water

Steam sweet potatoes for 16-18 minutes, or until tender.

Steam green beans for 4-6 minutes, or until tender.

Blend sweet potatoes, green beans, and water until desired consistency is achieved.

*Appropriate age: 8-10 months

*Servings: 10-12

*Cooking time: 16-18 minutes

*Able to freeze

Sweet Potato Corn

2 medium-sized sweet potatoes (peeled and chopped)

1 cup frozen peas or 1 cup fresh peas (removed from pod)

3 ears of corn (cut kernels from cob) or 1 cup frozen corn kernels

1 tablespoon water

Steam sweet potatoes for 16-18 minutes, or until tender.

Steam peas for 4-6 minutes, or until tender.

Blend sweet potatoes, peas, corn, and water until desired consistency is achieved.

*Appropriate age: 8-10 months

*Servings: 12+

*Cooking time: 16-18 minutes

*Able to freeze

Sweet Potato and Brown Rice

1 medium-sized sweet potato (peeled and chopped)

¼ cup brown rice

1 tablespoon water

Steam sweet potato for 16-18 minutes, or until tender.

Cook rice in boiling water for 5 minutes. Reduce heat and simmer for 15 minutes, or until rice is tender.

Blend sweet potato, brown rice, and water until desired consistency is achieved.

*Appropriate age: 8-10 months

*Servings: 8-10

*Cooking time: 20 minutes

*Unable to freeze

Sweet Savory Veggies

1 medium-sized sweet potato (peeled and chopped)

1 medium-sized white potato (peeled and chopped)

3 to 4 broccoli florets (quartered)

1 tablespoon water

Steam sweet potato for 16-18 minutes, or until tender.

Steam white potato for 16-18 minutes, or until tender.

Steam broccoli for 4-6 minutes.

Blend sweet potato, white potato, broccoli, and water until desired consistency is achieved.

*Appropriate age: 10-12 months

*Servings: 10-12

*Cooking time: 16-18 minutes

*Able to freeze

Sweet Potato Chicken

1 medium-sized sweet potato (peeled and chopped)

1 chicken breast (boneless, skinless)

1 tablespoon water

Steam sweet potato for 16-18 minutes, or until tender.

Cook chicken in boiling water for 12-14 minutes, or until thoroughly cooked.

Blend sweet potato, chicken, and water until desired consistency is achieved.

*Appropriate age: 8-10 months

*Servings: 8-10

*Cooking time: 16-18 minutes

*Able to freeze

Sweet Apple Chicken

1 medium-sized sweet potato (peeled and chopped)

1 apple (peeled, cored, and chopped)

1 chicken breast (boneless, skinless)

1 tablespoon water

Steam sweet potatoes for 16-18 minutes, or until tender.

Steam apple for 5-7 minutes, or until tender.

Cook chicken in boiling water for 12-14 minutes, or until thoroughly cooked.

Blend sweet potato, apple, chicken, and water until desired consistency is achieved.

*Appropriate age: 8-10 months

*Servings: 12+

*Cooking time: 16-18 minutes

*Able to freeze

Mash Potatoes

1 medium-sized white potato (peeled and chopped)

¼ cup water or ¼ cup breast milk/baby's milk supplement

1 tablespoon unsalted butter for taste (optional)

Steam white potato for 16-18 minutes, or until tender.

Blend potato, water or milk, and butter, if using, until desired consistency is achieved.

*Appropriate age: 6 months

*Servings: 2-3

*Cooking time: 16-18 minutes

*Able to freeze

Potatoes are a good source of potassium and vitamins B and C.

Butternut Mashed Taters

3 medium-sized white potatoes (peeled and chopped)

½ butternut squash (peeled, seeded, and cubed)

2 tablespoons water

Steam potatoes for 16-18 minutes, or until tender.

Steam squash for 6-8 minutes, or until tender.

Blend potatoes, squash, and water until desired consistency is achieved.

*Appropriate age: 6-8 months

*Servings: 12+

*Cooking time: 16-18 minutes

*Able to freeze

Potato Corn Bake

1 medium-sized white potato (peeled and chopped)

3 ears of corn (cut kernels from cob) or 1 cup frozen corn kernels

¼ cup water or ¼ cup breast milk/baby's milk supplement

Steam potato for 16-18 minutes, or until tender.

Steam corn for 8-10 minutes, or until tender.

Blend potato, corn, and water or milk until desired consistency is achieved.

*Appropriate age: 10-12 months

*Servings: 8-10

*Cooking time: 16-18 minutes

*Able to freeze

White Potato with Peas

1 medium-sized white potato (peeled and chopped)

1 cup frozen peas or 1 cup fresh peas (removed from pod)

2 tablespoons water

Steam potato for 16-18 minutes, or until tender.

Steam peas for 8-10 minutes, or until tender.

Blend potato, peas, and water until desired consistency is achieved.

*Appropriate age: 8-10 months

*Servings: 2

*Cooking time: 16-18 minutes

*Able to freeze

White Potato and Green Beans

2 medium-sized white potatoes (peeled and chopped)

1 cup frozen green beans or 1 cup fresh green beans (topped, tailed, and chopped)

¼ cup water or ¼ cup breast milk/baby's milk supplement

Steam potatoes for 16-18 minutes, or until tender.

Steam green beans for 4-6 minutes, or until tender.

Blend potatoes, green beans, and water or milk until desired consistency is achieved.

*Appropriate age: 8-10 months

*Servings: 10-12

*Cooking time: 16-18 minutes

*Able to freeze

Chicken and Taties

2 medium-sized white potatoes (peeled and chopped)

1 chicken breast (boneless, skinless)

2 tablespoons water

Steam potatoes for 16-18 minutes, or until tender.

Cook chicken in boiling water for 12-14 minutes, or until cooked thoroughly.

Blend potatoes, chicken, and water until desired consistency is achieved.

*Appropriate age: 8-10 months

*Servings: 10-12

*Cooking time: 16-18 minutes

*Able to freeze

Tasty Taters

2 medium-sized white potatoes (peeled and chopped)

1 cup frozen peas or 1 cup fresh peas (removed from pod)

3 ears of corn (cut kernels from cob) or 1 cup frozen corn kernels

2 tablespoons water

Steam potatoes for 16-18 minutes or until tender.

Place peas and corn in steamer and steam for 8-10 minutes, or until tender.

Blend potatoes, peas, corn, and water until desired consistency is achieved.

*Appropriate age: 8-10 months

*Servings: 12+

*Cooking time: 16-18 minutes

*Able to freeze

Summer Squash Puree

1 yellow squash (trimmed and chopped)

2 tablespoons water

Steam squash for 6-8 minutes, or until tender.

Blend yellow squash and water until desired consistency is achieved.

*Appropriate age: 8-10 months

*Servings: 6-8

*Cooking time: 6-8 minutes

*Able to freeze

Zucchini squash can be substituted for yellow squash

Yellow Squash is a very good source of dietary fiber, protein, vitamin A, B, C, folate, iron, magnesium, phosphorus, potassium, zinc, and manganese.

Summer Squash with Peas

1 yellow squash (trimmed and chopped)

1 cup frozen peas or 1 cup fresh peas (removed from pod)

2 tablespoons water

Steam squash for 6-8 minutes, or until tender.

Steam peas for 8-10 minutes, or until tender

Blend squash, peas, and water until desired consistency is achieved.

*Appropriate age: 8-10 months

*Servings: 12+

*Cooking time: 8-10 minutes

*Able to freeze

Squish Squash Green Bean

1 yellow squash (trimmed and chopped)

1 cup frozen green beans or 1 cup fresh green beans (topped, tailed, and chopped)

2 tablespoons water

Steam squash for 6-8 minutes, or until tender

Steam green beans for 8-10 minutes, or until tender

Blend yellow squash, green beans, and water until desired consistency is achieved.

*Appropriate age: 8-10 months

*Servings: 12+

*Cooking time: 8-10 minutes

*Able to freeze

Yummy Yellow Squash Chicken

1 yellow squash (trimmed and chopped)

1 chicken breast (boneless, skinless)

2 tablespoons water or 2 tablespoons unsweetened apple juice for taste (optional)

Steam squash for 6-8 minutes, or until tender

Cook chicken in boiling water for 12-14 minutes, or until cooked thoroughly.

Blend squash, chicken, and water until desired consistency is achieved. Stir in apple juice, if using.

*Appropriate age: 8-10 months

*Servings: 10-12

*Cooking time: 12-14 minutes

*Able to freeze

Summer Squash and Brown Rice

1 yellow squash (trimmed and chopped)

¼ cup brown rice

2 tablespoons water

Steam yellow squash for 8-10 minutes, or until tender.

Cook rice in boiling water for 5 minutes. Reduce heat and simmer for 15 minutes, or until rice is tender.

Blend squash, brown rice, and water until desired consistency is achieved.

*Appropriate age: 8-10 months

*Servings: 10-12

*Cooking time: 20 minutes

*Unable to freeze

Squashy Noodle

1 yellow squash (trimmed and chopped)

½ cup dry pasta (of choice)

2 tablespoons water

Steam squash for 6-8 minutes, or until tender

Cook pasta in boiling water for 8-10 minutes, or until tender. Drain excess water.

Blend squash, pasta, and water until desired consistency is achieved.

*Appropriate age: 8-10 months

*Servings: 8-10

*Cooking time: 8-10 minutes

*Unable to freeze

CPSIA information can be obtained at www.ICGtesting.com
Printed in the USA
LVOW051100091111

254199LV00001B/151/P